# MACHINES CLOSE-UP

# MODERN WARSHIPS & SUBMARINES

## David West and Alex Pang

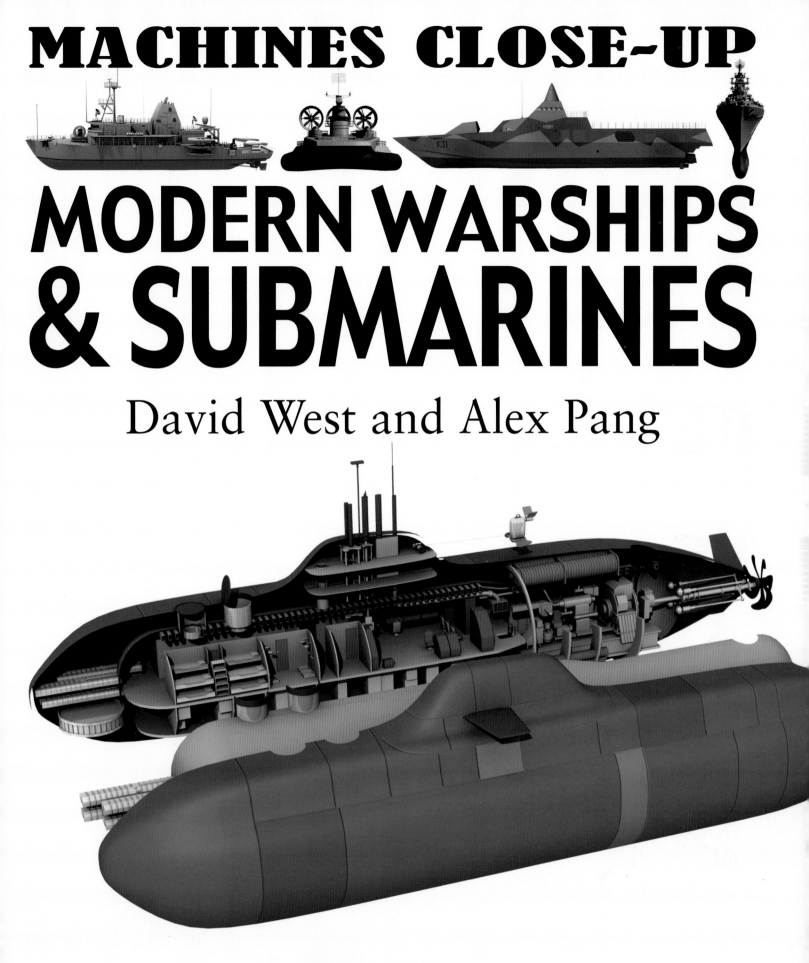

 **Marshall Cavendish**
Benchmark

New York

This edition first published in 2011 in the United States by
Marshall Cavendish Benchmark

An imprint of Marshall Cavendish Corporation

Website: www.marshallcavendish.us

This publication represents the opinions and views of the author based on
Daniel Gilpin's and Alex Pang's personal experience, knowledge, and
research. The information in this book serves as a general guide only. The
author and publisher have used their best efforts in preparing this book and
disclaim liability rising directly and indirectly from the use and application of
this book.

Other Marshall Cavendish Offices:
Marshall Cavendish International (Asia) Private Limited, 1 New Industrial
Road, Singapore 536196 • Marshall Cavendish International (Thailand) Co
Ltd. 253 Asoke, 12th Flr, Sukhumvit 21 Road, Klongtoey Nua, Wattana,
Bangkok 10110, Thailand • Marshall Cavendish (Malaysia) Sdn Bhd, Times
Subang, Lot 46, Subang Hi-Tech Industrial Park, Batu Tiga, 40000 Shah
Alam, Selangor Darul Ehsan, Malaysia

Marshall Cavendish is a trademark of Times Publishing Limited

Copyright © 2009 David West Children's Books

Library of Congress Cataloging-in-Publication Data

Gilpin, Daniel.
Modern warships & submarines / Daniel Gilpin and Alex Pang.
p. cm. -- (Machines close-up)
Originally published: London : Wayland, 2009.
Summary: "Reveals and discusses the intricate internal workings of modern
warships and submarines"--Provided by publisher.
Includes index.
ISBN 978-1-60870-110-0
1. Warships--Juvenile literature. 2. Submarines (Ships)--Juvenile literature.
I. Pang, Alex. II. Title. III. Title: Modern warships and submarines.
V765.G54 2011
623.825--dc22
2009043258

First published in 2009 by Wayland
Hachette Children's Books
338 Euston Road
London NW1 3BH
Wayland Australia
Level 17/207 Kent Street
Sydney, NSW 2000

Produced by
David West ⚇ Children's Books
7 Princeton Court
55 Felsham Road
London SW15 1AZ

Editor: Katharine Pethick
Designer: Gary Jeffrey
Illustrator: Alex Pang
Consultant: Steve Parker

The photographs in this book are used by permission and through the
courtesy of:
Abbreviations: t-top, m-middle, b-bottom, r-right,
l-left, c-center.
4-5, PH3 ALTA I. CUTLER; USN; 8b, junmon603; 9tl,
Bundesarchiv; 9b, DoD photo by Petty Officer 3rd Class
Christopher Mobley, U.S. Navy; 30t, U.S. Navy Photo;
30l, MC1 Brien Aho, U.S. Navy Photographer; 30b, U.S.
Navy Photo

Printed in China
135642

# CONTENTS

4 INTRODUCTION

6 RAIDERS AND TRADERS

8 SEA POWER

10 BALLISTIC MISSILE SUBMARINE

12 FAST ATTACK SUBMARINE

14 DIESEL-ELECTRIC SUBMARINE

**16 AIRCRAFT CARRIER**

**24 LITTORAL COMBAT SHIP**

**18 CRUISER**

**26 AMPHIBIOUS ASSAULT CRAFT**

**20 DESTROYER**

**28 MINE HUNTER-KILLER**

**22 STEALTH CORVETTE**

**30 FUTURE MACHINES**

**31 GLOSSARY**

**32 INDEX**

Glossary Words: when a word is printed in **bold**, you can look up its meaning in the Glossary on page 31.

# INTRODUCTION

Modern warships and submarines are packed with the most amazing pieces of war hardware and software. From ground-hugging, submarine-launched cruise missiles to five-thousand-round-ammunition Gatling guns, these are the most expensive of all weapons of war.

*WARSHIP FLEET*
*A parade of modern warships shows the usual ships in a fleet. The aircraft carriers are the **capital ships** and are protected by **frigates**, destroyers, and unseen attack submarines.*

# HOW TO USE THIS BOOK

## MAIN TEXT
Explains the history of the ship and outlines its primary role.

## SPECIFICATIONS
Gives information about the ship's speed, dimensions, and personnel.

## MAIN ILLUSTRATION
Shows the internal structure of the ship and gives information on the positions of its various working parts.

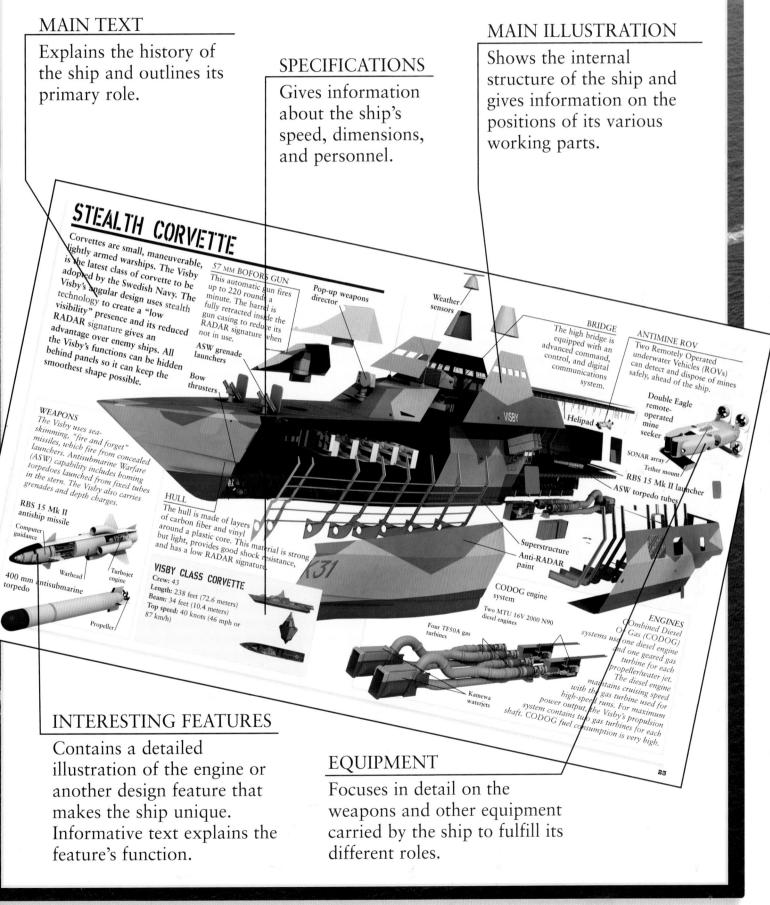

### STEALTH CORVETTE

Corvettes are small, maneuverable, lightly armed warships. The Visby is the latest class of corvette to be adopted by the Swedish Navy. The Visby's angular design uses stealth technology to create a "low visibility" presence and its reduced RADAR signature gives an advantage over enemy ships. All the Visby's functions can be hidden behind panels so it can keep the smoothest shape possible.

**57 MM BOFORS GUN**
This automatic gun fires up to 220 rounds a minute. The barrel is fully retracted inside the gun casing to reduce its RADAR signature when not in use.

**ASW grenade launchers**

Pop-up weapons director

Weather sensors

**BRIDGE**
The high bridge is equipped with an advanced command, control, and digital communications system.

**ANTIMINE ROV**
Two Remotely Operated underwater Vehicles (ROVs) can detect and dispose of mines safely, ahead of the ship.

Bow thrusters

Double Eagle remote-operated mine seeker

VISBY

Helipad

SONAR array

Tether mount

RBS 15 Mk II launcher

ASW torpedo tubes

**WEAPONS**
The Visby uses sea-skimming, "fire and forget" missiles, which fire from concealed launchers. Antisubmarine Warfare (ASW) capability includes homing torpedoes launched from fixed tubes in the stern. The Visby also carries grenades and depth charges.

**RBS 15 Mk II antiship missile**

Computer guidance

Warhead

Turbojet engine

400 mm antisubmarine torpedo

Propeller

**HULL**
The hull is made of layers of carbon fiber and vinyl around a plastic core. This material is strong but light, provides good shock resistance, and has a low RADAR signature.

**VISBY CLASS CORVETTE**
Crew: 43
Length: 238 feet (72.6 meters)
Beam: 34 feet (10.4 meters)
Top speed: 40 knots (46 mph or 87 km/h)

K31

Superstructure

Anti-RADAR paint

**CODOG engine system**

Two MTU 16V 2000 N90 diesel engines

Four TF50A gas turbines

Kamewa waterjets

**ENGINES**
COmbined Diesel Or Gas (CODOG) systems use one diesel engine and one geared gas turbine for each propeller/water jet. The diesel engine maintains cruising speed with the gas turbine used for high-speed runs. For maximum power output, the Visby's propulsion system contains two gas turbines for each shaft. CODOG fuel consumption is very high.

22

23

## INTERESTING FEATURES
Contains a detailed illustration of the engine or another design feature that makes the ship unique. Informative text explains the feature's function.

## EQUIPMENT
Focuses in detail on the weapons and other equipment carried by the ship to fulfill its different roles.

# RAIDERS AND TRADERS

**W**arships were probably created when pirates began raiding merchant ships. Especially fast, slim ships with armed men onboard were sent to protect valuable sea trading routes.

## GALLEYS

In the time of ancient Greece and the Roman Empire, the most common type of warship was the galley—a long, narrow vessel powered by groups of oarsmen. Carrying armed men, it could ram and sink enemy vessels, or come alongside enemy forces and attack them. Viking longships were ideal for raiding coastal waters due to their shallow depth.

### BIREME
*The bireme, a galley with two banks of oars, was an eighth century warship. Some galleys had up to five banks of oars.*

### VIKING LONGSHIP

### VENETIAN GALLEY
*Fighting galleys were used well into the sixteenth century in the Mediterranean Sea.*

### TUDOR FLAGSHIP
*The* Mary Rose, *a sixteenth century carrack, had ninety-one guns.*

## SAILS AND CANNONS

By the fifteenth century, warships were carrying cannons. Carracks were large, oceangoing ships with three or four masts. These evolved into speedy galleons—warships that dominated sea battles.

### GALLEON
*The Spanish galleon was the ultimate man-o'-war during the early seventeenth century.*

## SHIPS OF THE LINE

Since the seventeenth century, warships carried large numbers of cannon on each side. Ships formed a line of battle to fire at each other's **broadsides**—the tactic that gave the ships their name. These ships of the line carried up to 140 guns on two or three decks. The fleets with the heaviest broadsides usually won.

**BROADSIDE**
*As seen in this eighteenth century warship broadside, battles were decided by which ship had the most guns.*

**USS CONSTITUTION**
*The wooden-hulled USS* Constitution *defeated five British warships in 1812 and is the oldest commissioned naval vessel still afloat. It was built in the 1790s.*

## STEAM AND STEEL

From the mid–nineteenth century, the sailing ships of the line were replaced by metal-hulled, steam-powered battleships, while the sailing frigates were replaced by steam-powered cruisers. With the invention of rotating **turrets**, the guns could be aimed independently of the ship's direction.

**ARMORED CRUISER**
*Launched in 1887, Dupuy de Lôme was a forerunner of the twentieth century dreadnoughts.*

**IRONCLAD CLASH**
*The first real battle between armored ships took place during the Civil War.*

# SEA POWER

**BRANDTAUCHER**
Brandtaucher *was a German submersible ship built in 1850—one of the first military submarines.*

**I**n 1904, Britain's First Sea Lord, Sir John Fisher, was convinced of the need for fast, powerful ships. Fisher's concern was the submarines and destroyers that were equipped with torpedoes and had a greater range than battleship guns.

## DREADNOUGHTS AND CARRIERS

Fisher's answer was the battle cruiser dreadnought, heavily armed with ten 305 mm guns and the first warship to be propelled to 21 knots (24 mph or 39 km/h) by steam turbines. During World War I, however, the great dreadnought fleets were less effective than expected, as the threats to battleships from submarines, mines, and torpedoes were too great without protection from destroyers. With the invention of **fixed-wing aircraft** in 1903, navies were soon launching planes from warships.

**U-BOAT**
*By 1918, thousands of tons of Allied forces' ships had been sunk by the German U-boats (submarines) during World War I.*

**HMS DREADNOUGHT**
*In 1906, the HMS* Dreadnought *revolutionized naval power. The resulting arms race created monsters like the USS* Texas, *built in 1912.*

**FLAT TOP**
*In 1918, HMS Argus was the world's first full-length, flat-deck aircraft carrier.*

## BISMARCK

Bismarck—*perhaps the most famous ship of World War II—was ultimately defeated by a carrier-borne aircraft.*

## *USS* FORRESTAL

*This 1950s ship was one of the first carriers to feature an angled landing deck with a straight take-off deck.*

## TICONDEROGA

*The U.S. Ticonderoga class cruiser is a typical modern warship using guided missiles rather than guns for its main armament.*

## LAST GREAT NAVAL WAR

By the beginning of World War II, it had become clear that aircraft carriers were the leading ships of the fleet and that battleships now performed a secondary role. The Battle of the Atlantic was fought between destroyers and submarines, and most of the decisive fleet clashes of the Pacific war were determined by aircraft carriers.

## MODERN NAVIES

Modern warships are generally divided into seven main categories: aircraft carriers, cruisers, destroyers, frigates, corvettes, submarines, and amphibious assault craft. Each category has its own role in a modern navy.

## TYPHOON

*This Soviet **ballistic missile** launcher was the largest class of submarine ever built.*

# BALLISTIC MISSILE SUBMARINE

Ballistic missile submarines are equipped to launch long-range, rocket-powered missiles. These massive submarines prowl the ocean depths as movable missile platforms, keeping as quiet as possible. They have two crews, each on duty for one hundred days.

SAIL/FIN
The sail or fin houses the **conning tower**, the periscopes, **RADAR** (RAdio Detection And Ranging), and communications masts or antenna. It may also support the control surfaces that steer the submarine up or down.

Submarine-Launched Ballistic Missile

Periscope

RADAR and radio antennae

Launch hatch

Control surface

Control room

Periscope

Water-filled nose cone

Crew quarters

Torpedo tubes

SONAR

*CONTROL ROOM*
*This large, well-lit room holds the controls for most of the sub's vital operations, including periscopes, navigation (which uses the **Global Positioning System** [GPS]), large plotting tables, steering, ballast control, and weapons control.*

SONAR
Submarines use passive **SONAR** (SOund Navigation And Ranging) to listen for the enemy. Active SONAR sends pulses of sound that give away the submarine's position.

## MISSILE LAUNCH TUBES

The submarine has twenty-four Trident Submarine-Launched Ballistic Missile (SLBM) tubes that launch missiles 50 meters below the surface so the submarine remains undetected from the air. The latest missiles have multiple warheads.

## POWER PLANT

Powered by a **nuclear reactor**, the submarine can stay underwater without the need to refuel. It has an auxiliary diesel engine in case the nuclear reactor has to be shut down.

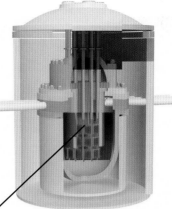

Reactor core

**Pressurized water reactor**

Propeller

Auxiliary diesel engine

Pressure hull

### TRIDENT II

*Launched underwater, the SLBM three-stage, solid-fuel rocket motor delivers eight Multiple Independently targetable Reentry Vehicles (MIRVs), each carrying a nuclear warhead.*

Warheads

Stage 3

Stage 2

Stage 1

726

## OHIO CLASS SUBMARINE

**Crew:** 155
**Length:** 557 feet (170 meters)
**Beam:** 42 feet (13 meters)
**Speed:** 25 knots (28 mph or 46 km/h) submerged
**Depth Capability:** 300 meters

## OUTER HULL AND PRESSURE HULL

The external hull is 42 feet and is 2 to 4 millimeters thick. It has the same pressure on both sides. Inside the outer hull is the pressure hull, which contains the living areas and withstands the outside water pressure.

# FAST ATTACK SUBMARINE

These nuclear-powered submarines seek and destroy the enemy's submarines and surface ships. They can also attack targets on land with Tomahawk cruise missiles, carry Special Operation forces, perform Intelligence, Surveillance, and Reconnaissance (ISR) missions and engage in mine warfare.

## LOS ANGELES CLASS SUBMARINE

Crew: 127
Length: 360 feet (110 meters)
Beam: 32 feet (10 meters)
Top speed: 33 knots (38 mph or 61 km/h) submerged
Depth Capability: 290 meters

## MULTIPLE LAUNCH TUBES

Twelve vertical launch system tubes fire the Tomahawk cruise missiles. Ejected by gas pressure, the missiles exit the water and a rocket is ignited for the first few seconds of airborne flight until the wings unfold and the turbofan engine can be used.

SONAR

Turbofan engine

Wings

Airscoop

**Tomahawk cruise missile**

## TORPEDO TUBES

Torpedoes, antiship missiles, and even Tomahawk cruise missiles can be launched from the torpedo tubes.

## CRUISE MISSILE

The missile's wings unfold for flight, the **airscoop** is exposed, and the turbofan engine is employed for cruising. Over water, the Tomahawk uses **inertial guidance** or GPS to follow a preset course.

Twin turbine and
auxiliary diesel engine

Diesel engine

Propeller

Turbine

## PROPULSION SYSTEMS

*The submarine relies on nuclear power for both propulsion and life support. The nuclear reactor heats water that makes steam, which drives a turbine to turn the propeller. The same system also provides steam for the boat's turbine generators—the source of electricity for all submarine systems.*

Guidance fins

## BALLAST TANKS

Ballast tanks are used to allow the vessel to submerge, taking water in to allow the submarine to dive. When the submarine surfaces, water is blown out from the tanks using compressed air.

Nuclear reactor

## MANEUVERING ROOM

The maneuvering room controls the nuclear reactor and converts its heat to energy for powering the submarine's systems and propulsion.

## WEAPONS

*Mk 48 torpedoes can be guided from a submarine by wires attached to the torpedo. They can also use their own active or passive sensors. A capsule containing the Harpoon antiship missile can also be fired from the torpedo tubes.*

Harpoon antiship
missile

Rocket engine

Piston engine

Pump-jet

Fuel

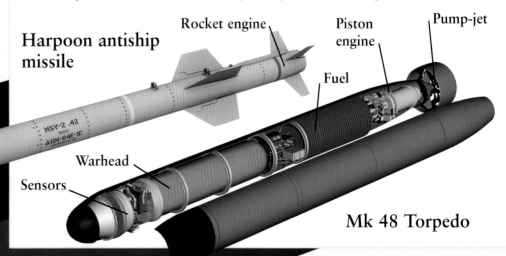

Warhead

Sensors

Mk 48 Torpedo

# DIESEL-ELECTRIC SUBMARINE

A diesel-electric submarine is a highly advanced nonnuclear submarine. It can operate at high speed on diesel power or switch to an electric power system for silent, slow cruising, and stay submerged for up to three weeks.

## CONTROL ROOM
Command and weapons control systems are monitored along with sensors, weapons, and navigation.

Sail

## LIVING QUARTERS
The area where the crew sleeps and eats is cramped. Every small space is used for storage.

Main SONAR

Batteries

Torpedo tubes

## WEAPONS
*There are six torpedo tubes in two groups of three. The Type 212 submarine uses a water ram expulsion system for launching torpedoes such as the Black Shark heavyweight torpedo, which has fiber-optic wire guidance. The short range Interactive Defense and Attack System (IDAS) missile is being developed to fire from Type 212's torpedo tubes.*

IDAS missile

Black Shark heavyweight torpedo

## TOWED SONAR ARRAY

SONAR devices can be towed behind a submarine to listen for enemy ships and submarines, so they have less interference from the noise of the submarine.

**Sonar device**

Stabilizer fins

## TYPE 212 U-BOAT
**Crew:** 23-27
**Length:** 183 feet (56 meters)
**Beam:** 30 feet (7 meters)
**Top speed:** 20 knots (23 mph or 37 km/h) submerged
**Depth Capability:** over 700 meters

Oxygen supply

## OUTER HULL

On modern military submarines the outer hull is covered with a layer of sound-absorbing rubber to reduce detection.

Prop motor

Hydrogen

## PROPULSION SYSTEMS

*The Type 212 is propelled by a diesel engine and an additional Air-Independent Propulsion (AIP) system that uses hydrogen* **fuel cells.** *Stored in tanks between the pressure hull and outer light hull, the hydrogen and oxidizer are piped through the pressure hull to the fuel cells when electricity is needed. The fuel cell system has nine fuel cells, each of which provides between 30 and 50 kilowatts of electricity.*

**Combination diesel or fuel cell/electric system**

Oxygen

Fuel cells

Diesel generator

Fuel cells

Diesel engine

Propeller

Inner hull

Hydrogen

# AIRCRAFT CARRIER

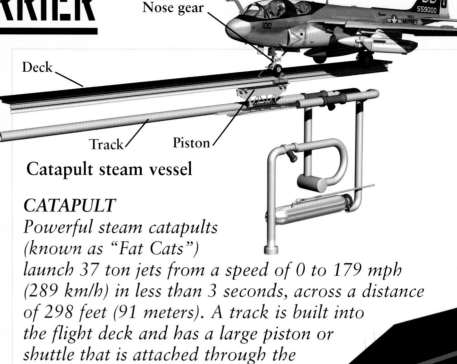

Aircraft carriers allow a naval force to provide air power at great distances without having to depend on land bases. The Nimitz class super-carriers, a line of nuclear-powered aircraft carriers in service with the U.S. Navy, are the largest warships in the world. Each displaces over 100,000 tons of water fully loaded.

Nose gear

Deck

Track    Piston

**Catapult steam vessel**

*CATAPULT*
*Powerful steam catapults (known as "Fat Cats") launch 37 ton jets from a speed of 0 to 179 mph (289 km/h) in less than 3 seconds, across a distance of 298 feet (91 meters). A track is built into the flight deck and has a large piston or shuttle that is attached through the track to the nose gear of the aircraft.*

## FLIGHT DECK
The flight deck is divided into two runways. One has a catapult and is used for takeoff; the other sits at an angle and is used for landing.

## CREW QUARTERS
About sixty personnel share a compartment, sleeping in single bunks, called "racks," built together in stacks of three.

## ISLAND

This is the command center for the flight deck and all ship operations. About 151 feet (46 meters) tall, but narrow at the base, the island takes up little space on the flight deck.

## HANGER DECK

When they are not in use, most of the eighty-five aircraft are secured in the hangar bay. The bay is more than two-thirds the length of the ship.

## NIMITZ CLASS CARRIER

**Crew:** 5,680
**Length:** 1,092 feet (332.8 meters)
**Beam:** 249 feet (76.8 meters)
**Top speed:** 30 knots (34.5 mph or 56 km/h)

## POWER PLANT

*The carrier's two nuclear reactors give unlimited range and endurance, and a top speed in excess of 30 knots (34.5 mph or 56 km/h). Eight steam turbine generators each produce 8,000 kilowatts of electrical power—enough to serve a small city.*

**Nuclear reactors and steam turbines**

Nuclear reactor

Propellers

Steam turbines

# CRUISER

The Kirov class cruisers are the largest and most powerful warships in the Russian Navy, second only to aircraft carriers. Similar in size to World War I battleships, they are referred to as large missile cruisers by the Russian Navy. Commissioned in the 1980s, only four were completed.

## KIROV CLASS CRUISER *ADMIRAL NAKHIMOV*

Crew: 727
Length: 827 feet (252 meters)
Beam: 93.5 feet (28.5 meters)
Top speed: 30 knots (34.5 mph or 56 km/h)

## CRUISE MISSILE LAUNCHERS

The main weapons are twenty Shipwreck cruise missiles that are mounted on deck and designed to engage enemy warships and Snowstorm antisubmarine missiles.

Shipwreck cruise missile

SAM 9 launchers

Hull bulb

Waterline

## AIR DEFENSE MISSILES

Twelve launchers and ninety-six vertical launch air defense missiles can engage both air and surface targets.

## HULL

The size of the ship means there is plenty of space for command, control, and communications.

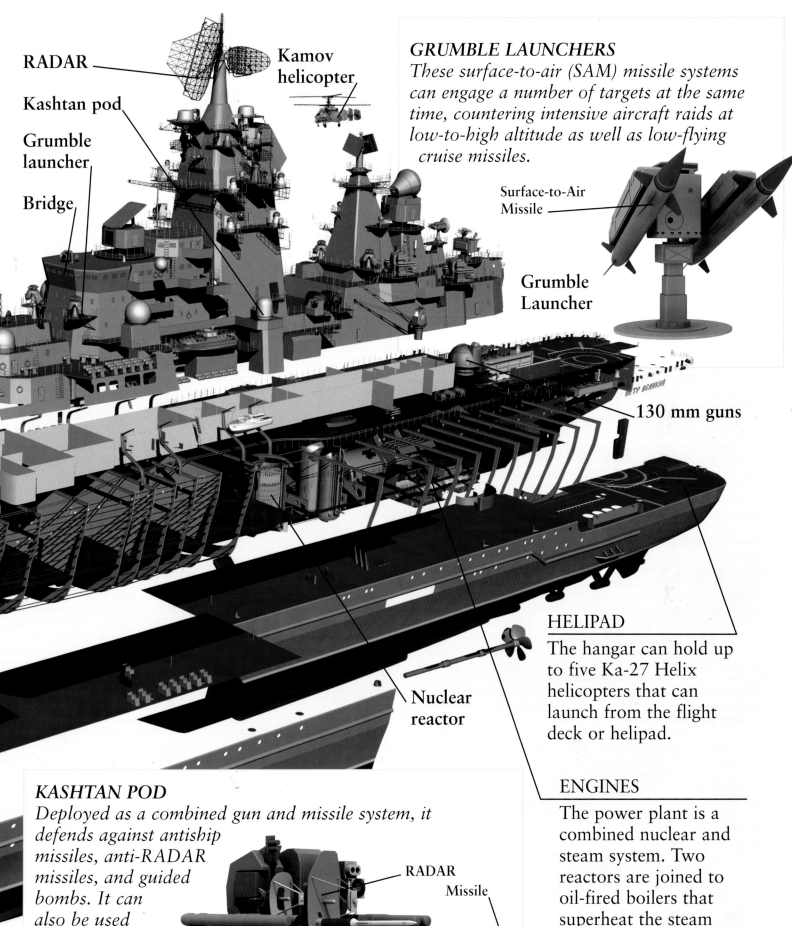

RADAR

Kashtan pod

Grumble launcher

Bridge

Kamov helicopter

## GRUMBLE LAUNCHERS
*These surface-to-air (SAM) missile systems can engage a number of targets at the same time, countering intensive aircraft raids at low-to-high altitude as well as low-flying cruise missiles.*

Surface-to-Air Missile

Grumble Launcher

130 mm guns

Nuclear reactor

## HELIPAD
The hangar can hold up to five Ka-27 Helix helicopters that can launch from the flight deck or helipad.

## KASHTAN POD
*Deployed as a combined gun and missile system, it defends against antiship missiles, anti-RADAR missiles, and guided bombs. It can also be used against aircraft and fast attack boats.*

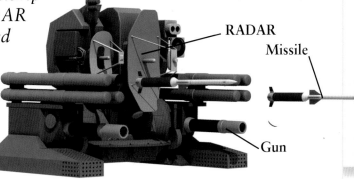

RADAR

Missile

Gun

## ENGINES
The power plant is a combined nuclear and steam system. Two reactors are joined to oil-fired boilers that superheat the steam produced in the reactor to increase the power for high speeds.

# DESTROYER

Also known as guided missile destroyers, the main role of modern destroyers is to protect larger vessels, such as aircraft carriers, from attacks by aircraft. Other operational jobs range from humanitarian relief to antidrug and embargo operations. Frigates have a similar job but specialize in antiship and antisubmarine warfare.

## MULTI-FUNCTION RADAR

*To perform its role the destroyer relies on a sophisticated RADAR system. The multi-function RADAR system detects all types of targets to a distance of 1,312 feet (400 kilometers). Able to track hundreds of targets at once, it is virtually immune to enemy jamming.*

Long distance RADAR

Lynx helicopter

RADAR

Crew bunks

30 mm gun

Mess area

T45

## ENGINES

The huge amount of electricity used by the ship's systems, and two electric propulsion motors, is supplied by two gas turbines.

## CREW AREAS

Cabins, messes, and recreational areas are suitable for male and female sailors. There is also space to board sixty marines and their equipment.

## BRIDGE

All ship operations are commanded from here.

## SUPERSTRUCTURE

The hull structure is made of 2,800 tons of steel. 40 tons of paint cover 1,076,391 square feet (100,000 square meters) of steel.

**Aster missile**

## MISSILE LAUNCHER

A mixture of shorter-range Aster 15 and longer-range Aster 30 missiles are launched from vertical launch silos. Each weighs almost as much as a small car.

**Vertical launch silo**

# TYPE 45 GUIDED MISSILE DESTROYER

**Crew:** 187-235
**Length:** 500 feet (152.4 meters)
**Beam:** 69.5 feet (21.2 meters)
**Top speed:** 29 knots (33 mph or 54 km/h)

*DEFENSES*

*The Type 45 has one large, long-distance gun and four smaller, "close-in" guns for final defense. The 114 mm naval gun can fire twenty-five rounds per minute with a range of 14 miles (22 kilometers). Two 30 mm auto guns are controlled by a joystick. Two Phalanx 20 mm auto guns are the final line of defense against antiship missiles. They search, detect, track, engage, and confirm kills, using their computer-controlled vertical launch silo RADAR system.*

**114 mm naval gun**

**30 mm auto gun**

**RADAR**

**Gun**

**Phalanx 20 mm auto gun**

# STEALTH CORVETTE

Corvettes are small, maneuverable, lightly armed warships. The Visby is the latest class of corvette to be adopted by the Swedish Navy. The Visby's angular design uses stealth technology to create a "low visibility" presence and its reduced RADAR signature gives an advantage over enemy ships. All the Visby's functions can be hidden behind panels so it can keep the smoothest shape possible.

## 57 MM BOFORS GUN

This automatic gun fires up to 220 rounds a minute. The barrel is fully retracted inside the gun casing to reduce its RADAR signature when not in use.

**ASW grenade launchers**

**Bow thrusters**

**Pop-up weapons director**

### WEAPONS

*The Visby uses sea-skimming, "fire and forget" missiles, which fire from concealed launchers. Antisubmarine Warfare (ASW) capability includes homing torpedoes launched from fixed tubes in the stern. The Visby also carries grenades and depth charges.*

**RBS 15 Mk II antiship missile**

Computer guidance

Warhead

Turbojet engine

**400 mm antisubmarine torpedo**

Propeller

## HULL

The hull is made of layers of carbon fiber and vinyl around a plastic core. This material is strong but light, provides good shock resistance, and has a low RADAR signature.

## VISBY CLASS CORVETTE

**Crew:** 43
**Length:** 238 feet (72.6 meters)
**Beam:** 34 feet (10.4 meters)
**Top speed:** 40 knots (46 mph or 87 km/h)

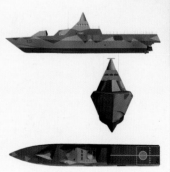

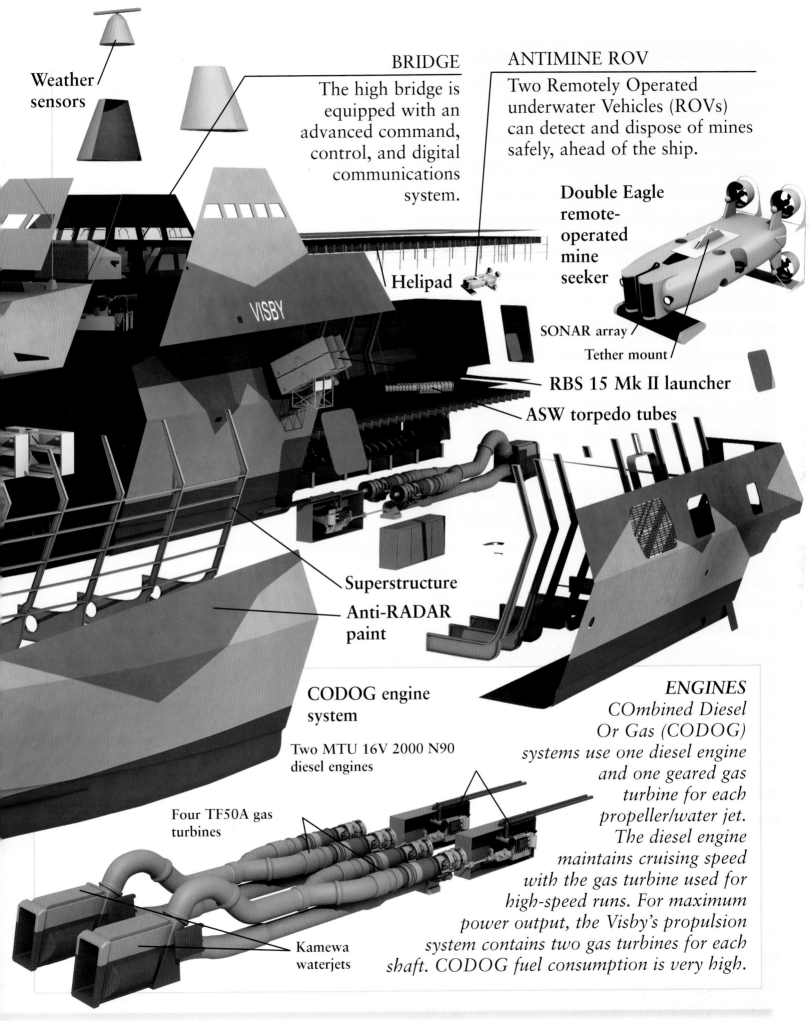

**Weather sensors**

**BRIDGE**
The high bridge is equipped with an advanced command, control, and digital communications system.

**ANTIMINE ROV**
Two Remotely Operated underwater Vehicles (ROVs) can detect and dispose of mines safely, ahead of the ship.

VISBY

Helipad

**Double Eagle remote-operated mine seeker**

SONAR array

Tether mount

RBS 15 Mk II launcher

ASW torpedo tubes

Superstructure

Anti-RADAR paint

CODOG engine system

Two MTU 16V 2000 N90 diesel engines

Four TF50A gas turbines

Kamewa waterjets

*ENGINES*
*COmbined Diesel Or Gas (CODOG) systems use one diesel engine and one geared gas turbine for each propeller/water jet. The diesel engine maintains cruising speed with the gas turbine used for high-speed runs. For maximum power output, the Visby's propulsion system contains two gas turbines for each shaft. CODOG fuel consumption is very high.*

# LITTORAL COMBAT SHIP

Littoral Combat Ships (LCS) are small surface vessels that operate in the littoral zone (close to shore). Equipped with a flight deck and hangar space for two Seahawk helicopters, they are used for assault transport. They can recover and launch small boats from a stern ramp and have enough cargo space to deliver an assault force with armored vehicles.

## 57 MM GUN

The Mk 110 57 mm gun is a multipurpose, medium caliber gun that can fire up to 220 rounds per minute, with a range of 8.7 miles (14 kilometers).

LOS mast

## RADAR

*Independence* has an integrated Line Of Sight (LOS) Mast, with **3-D RADAR** and a system that uses **infrared** to detect heat from enemy craft.

## HULL

The design for the *Independence* is based on a high-speed trimaran (three hulls), the *Benchijigua Express*, which is the largest trimaran in existence.

## BOW THRUSTER

This makes the ship more maneuverable in shallow waters and when docking.

## BRIDGE

The bridge is the control center of the ship. Beneath is the accommodation area for the crew and assault troops.

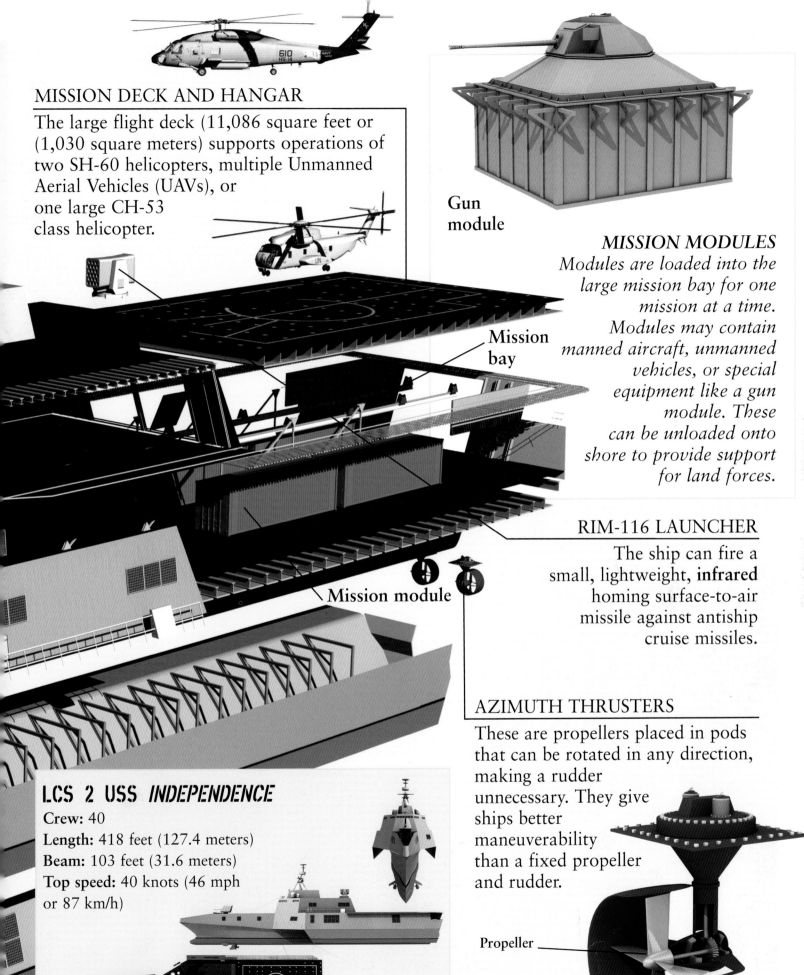

## MISSION DECK AND HANGAR

The large flight deck (11,086 square feet or (1,030 square meters) supports operations of two SH-60 helicopters, multiple Unmanned Aerial Vehicles (UAVs), or one large CH-53 class helicopter.

Gun module

*MISSION MODULES*

*Modules are loaded into the large mission bay for one mission at a time. Modules may contain manned aircraft, unmanned vehicles, or special equipment like a gun module. These can be unloaded onto shore to provide support for land forces.*

Mission bay

Mission module

## RIM-116 LAUNCHER

The ship can fire a small, lightweight, **infrared** homing surface-to-air missile against antiship cruise missiles.

## AZIMUTH THRUSTERS

These are propellers placed in pods that can be rotated in any direction, making a rudder unnecessary. They give ships better maneuverability than a fixed propeller and rudder.

Propeller

Pod

## LCS 2 USS *INDEPENDENCE*

**Crew:** 40
**Length:** 418 feet (127.4 meters)
**Beam:** 103 feet (31.6 meters)
**Top speed:** 40 knots (46 mph or 87 km/h)

# AMPHIBIOUS ASSAULT CRAFT

These high-speed, specialist craft are designed to sealift landing assault units, such as marines and tanks, from ship to shore, and to transport and plant mines. They are amphibious, meaning that they can travel over water or across beaches. They can go over walls that are up to 5 feet (1.6 meters) high.

## ZUBR AIR-CUSHIONED LANDING CRAFT

Crew: 31
Length: 187 feet (57 meters)
Draft: 5 feet (1.6 meters)
Top speed: 60 knots (69 mph or 111 km/h)

Strela-3

## DEFENSES

The ship has two Strela-3 multiple rocket launchers, four Igla-1M portable air defense missile systems, and two AK-630 30 mm automatic gun mounts. The six-barrel automatic gun can fire five thousand rounds per minute.

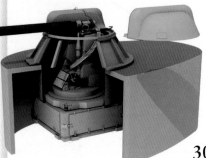

30 mm AK-630 gun pod

BTR-70 APC

T-80B tank

## HULL

The ship floats on a cushion of air trapped by a rubber skirt. The hull has light armor for protection from blast fragments.

Rubber skirt

## GENERATOR

The Zubr has two electric power plants. Each has two gas turbine generators supplying 100 kilowatts of electricity.

## PROPELLER MOTORS

*Three upright ring coverings house the air propellers at the back of the ship. These four-bladed propellers are driven by gas turbine engines.*

Electric motor

Ring covering

Air propeller

## TRANSPORT BAY

The Zubr can carry three battle tanks (such as the T-80B), eight BMP-2 infantry combat vehicles, ten BTR-70 armored personnel carriers (APC), or 360 equipped marines.

BMP-2

## CUSHION BLOWERS

*Four model NO-10 blowers generate the air cushion. The blowers are 8.2 feet (2.5 meters) in diameter. Air is sucked in from the top deck by the rotating fans, powered by gas turbine engines, to create a cushion of air.*

NO-10 blower

Gas turbine engine

Fan

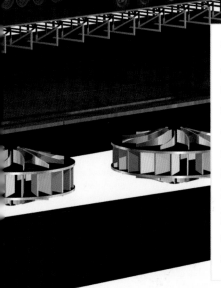

# MINE HUNTER-KILLER

These ships hunt out mines and destroy or neutralize them. Avenger class ships are mine hunter-killers capable of finding, classifying, and destroying moored mines.

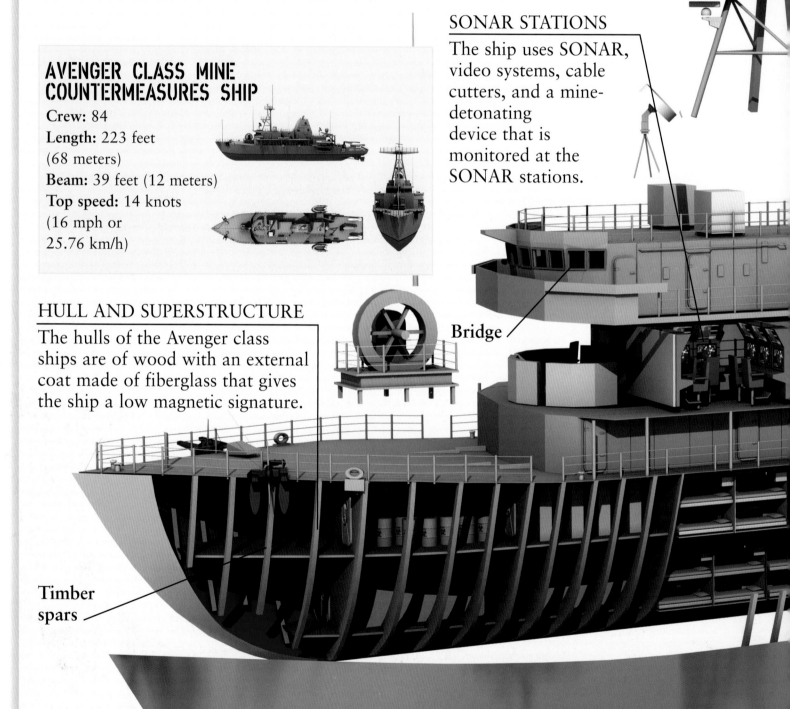

## AVENGER CLASS MINE COUNTERMEASURES SHIP

**Crew:** 84
**Length:** 223 feet (68 meters)
**Beam:** 39 feet (12 meters)
**Top speed:** 14 knots (16 mph or 25.76 km/h)

## SONAR STATIONS

The ship uses SONAR, video systems, cable cutters, and a mine-detonating device that is monitored at the SONAR stations.

Bridge

## HULL AND SUPERSTRUCTURE

The hulls of the Avenger class ships are of wood with an external coat made of fiberglass that gives the ship a low magnetic signature.

Timber spars

Fiberglass-coated plywood hull

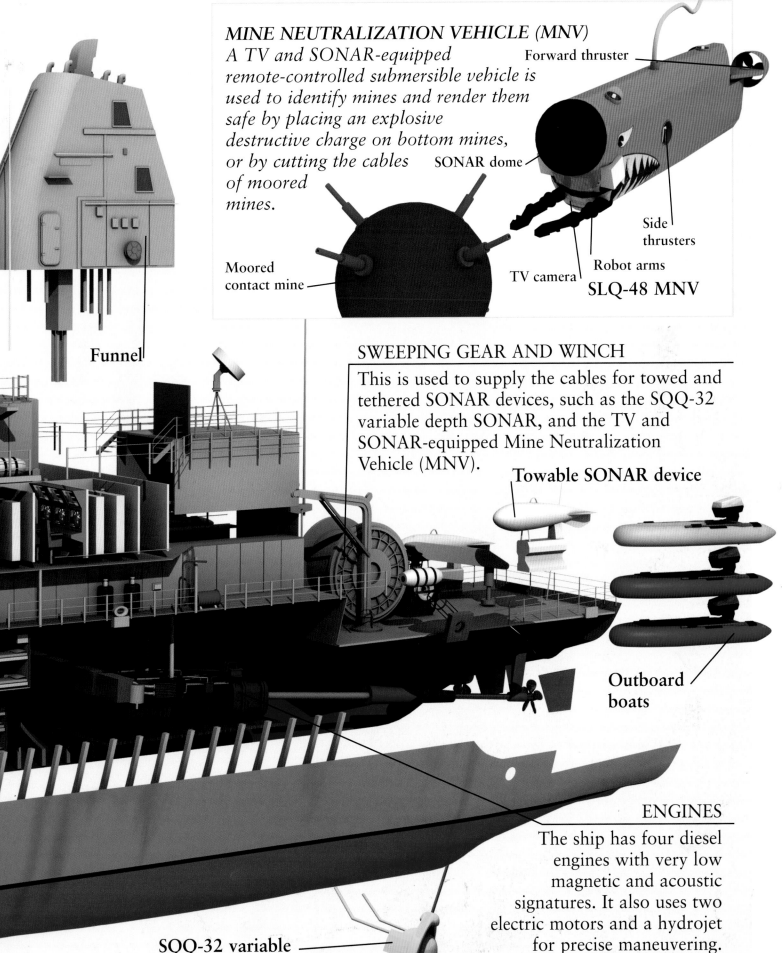

## MINE NEUTRALIZATION VEHICLE (MNV)

*A TV and SONAR-equipped remote-controlled submersible vehicle is used to identify mines and render them safe by placing an explosive destructive charge on bottom mines, or by cutting the cables of moored mines.*

Forward thruster

SONAR dome

Side thrusters

Moored contact mine

TV camera

Robot arms

**SLQ-48 MNV**

**Funnel**

## SWEEPING GEAR AND WINCH

This is used to supply the cables for towed and tethered SONAR devices, such as the SQQ-32 variable depth SONAR, and the TV and SONAR-equipped Mine Neutralization Vehicle (MNV).

**Towable SONAR device**

**Outboard boats**

## ENGINES

The ship has four diesel engines with very low magnetic and acoustic signatures. It also uses two electric motors and a hydrojet for precise maneuvering.

**SQQ-32 variable depth SONAR**

# FUTURE MACHINES

In the future, warships will differ fundamentally from today's vessels. They will be difficult to see due to anti-RADAR technology and difficult to hear as they will run on electric motors.

**FUTURE SUPERCARRIER**
*The Gerald R. Ford class aircraft carriers will be easier to maintain and more efficient during their fifty-year service life.*

Future warships may well be engineered as modular vessels consisting of several zones. If one zone gets severely damaged in an attack, automatic controls will instantaneously reroute the power to the rest of the ship. They will look very different from the ships of today. Stealth technology requires no right angles in the design and all weapons will be hidden away beneath smooth surfaces.

**USS FREEDOM**
*The prototype littoral combat ship USS Freedom is an alternative design to the USS Independence.*

**ZUMWALT**
*An artist's rendering of the Zumwalt class destroyer, a new class of multi-mission U.S. Navy surface combatant ship.*

# GLOSSARY

**3-D RADAR**
Provides an object's height, range, and direction. 2-D RADAR provides range and direction.

**airscoop**
A device that provides a noiseless, air-free heating, cooling, or combination system by separating out the air from the water in the system.

**ballistic missile**
A missile that follows a curved flight path to deliver a warhead (often nuclear) to an enemy target.

**broadside**
The side of a ship above the waterline.

**capital ship**
The most important warships in a navy's fleet.

**conning tower**
A raised structure on the deck of a submarine used for navigation and attack direction.

**embargo**
An official ban on trade with a particular country for political reasons.

**fixed-wing aircraft**
An airplane that is able to fly by using forward motion, which causes air to pass over its wings.

**fuel cell**
A fuel cell produces electricity from a fuel such as hydrogen and oxygen.

**frigate**
A modern warship that is smaller than a destroyer.

**Global Positioning System (GPS)**
A system of satellites that allows people with specialized receivers to pinpoint exactly where they are on the Earth.

**inertial guidance**
An electronic system that monitors position, speed, and acceleration, to provide navigational information without communicating with a base station.

**infrared**
Part of the electromagnetic spectrum (like light rays). Far infrared waves are thermal in the form of heat. Near infrared waves are shorter, not hot, and used by many devices, including TV remote controllers.

**nuclear reactor**
An enclosed vessel supplying energy for the generation of steam using controlled nuclear chain reactions.

**RAdio Detection And Ranging (RADAR)**
An object detection system that uses electromagnetic waves to identify the range, altitude, direction, and speed of objects.

**signature**
The amount a ship or other craft registers in a detection system such as RADAR or infrared. A low or small signature means it is hardly detectable.

**sealift**
Transport of military personnel and equipment by ship.

**SOund Navigation And Ranging (SONAR)**
A technique that uses sound (usually underwater) to navigate, communicate with, or detect other vessels. Active SONAR sends out sounds and listens to the "echo," while passive SONAR only "listens."

**stealth technology**
Also known as Low Observable (LO), this technology aims to make military craft less visible (or invisible) to RADAR, infrared, SONAR, and other detection methods.

**turbine**
A rotary engine with blades that are turned at high speed by steam or other hot gases. The rotation can be used to turn propellers or to power a generator to produce electricity.

**turret**
A revolving structure on a vehicle that protects the gunner and revolves to let the weapon be aimed in many directions.

# INDEX

Air-Independent Propulsion (AIP), 15
aircraft carrier, 2, 8, 9, 16, 18, 20, 30
anti-RADAR, 23, 30
Avenger class, 28
Azimuth thruster, 25

ballistic missile launcher, 9, 10, 11
Battle of the Atlantic, 9
battleship, 7, 8, 9, 18
bireme, 6
Black Shark, 14
BMP-2, 27
Bofors gun, 22
bow thruster, 22, 24
bridge, 19, 20, 23, 24, 26
broadsides, 7

cannon, 6, 7
carracks, 6
catapult, 16
Civil War, 7
COmbined Diesel Or Gas (CODOG), 23
Constitution, 7
control room, 10, 14
Corvette, 9, 22, 23
crew quarters, 10, 16
cruise missiles, 2, 12, 18, 19, 25
cruisers, 7, 8, 9, 18, 19

destroyer, 2, 8, 9, 20, 21, 30
diesel engine, 11, 13, 15, 23, 29
dreadnought, 7, 8
Dupuy de Lome, 7

Fisher, Sir John, 8
flagship, 6
fleet, 2, 7, 8, 9
flight deck, 16, 17, 19, 24, 25

frigate, 2, 7, 9, 20

galleon, 9
galley, 6
Gatling gun, 2
generator, 13, 15, 17, 27
Global Positioning System (GPS), 10, 12
grenade launcher, 22
grumble launcher, 19

Harpoon antiship missile, 13
HMS Argus, 8

Interactive Defense and Attack System (IDAS) missile, 14

Kamov helicopter, 19
Kashtan Pod, 19
Kirov, 18, 19

launch tubes, 11, 12
Littoral Combat Ship (LCS), 24, 25, 30
longship, 6
Line Of Sight (LOS) mast, 24
Lynx helicopter, 20

magnetic signature, 28
man-o'-war, 6
Mary Rose, 6
mines, 6, 9, 12, 23, 26, 28, 29
missile, 2, 9, 10, 11, 12, 13, 14, 18, 19, 20, 21, 22, 5, 26, 31
Mk 48, 13
Mk II, 22, 23
Multiple Independently targetable Reentry Vehicles (MIRV), 11

navy, 9, 15, 17, 22, 30
Nimitz, 16, 17

nuclear reactor, 11, 13, 17, 19, 31

Phalanx, 21
pirates, 6

RADAR, 10, 19, 20, 21, 22, 23, 24, 30
Remotely Operated underwater Vehicles (ROV), 23

sail, 6, 10, 14
Seahawk helicopter, 24
SONAR, 10, 12, 14, 15, 23, 28, 29, 21
steam turbines 8, 17
submarine, 2, 8, 9, 10, 11, 12, 13, 14, 15, 20, 22
Submarine-Launched Ballistic Missile (SLBM), 10, 11
supercarrier, 16, 20
superstructure, 21, 23, 28

torpedo, 8, 10, 12, 13, 14, 22, 23
Trident II, 11
turbofan engine, 12
Type 212, 14, 15
Type 45, 21
Typhoon, 9

U-boat, 8
Unmanned Aerial Vehicles (UAV), 25

Visby, 22, 23

warhead, 11, 13, 22, 31
warship, 2, 6, 7, 8, 9, 16, 18, 22, 30